MEAN *girls* GONE

a spiritual guide to getting rid of mean

Hayley DiMarco

pinkmosphere
a part of Hungry Planet

Revell
Grand Rapids, Michigan

Published by Fleming H. Revell
a division of Baker Publishing Group
P.O. Box 6287, Grand Rapids, MI 49516-6287

Printed in the United States of America

Library of Congress Cataloging-in-Publication Data is on file at the Library of Congress, Washington, DC.

ISBN 0-8007-3056-9

Published in association with Yates & Yates, LLP, Literary Agents, Orange, California.

Contents

Healing from the Inside Out

Finding Inner Peace in the Face of Mean

The End of the Journey

MEAN *girls* GONE

ANGEL
GOODY 2-SHOES
SWEET
NICE
COOL
CHATTY
VAIN
JEALOUS
NASTY
SHE-DEVIL
MEAN O METER
place hand here
TEST
YOURSELF!

Mean
Diagnosis

What it's all about

Mean Girls are everywhere. If you look hard enough, you'll find one under every rock. And they are there no matter what the age. From high school to middle age, they never seem to give up. In *Mean Girls: Facing Your Beauty Turned Beast*, I talked a lot about how to handle the Mean Girl in your life. But in *Mean Girls Gone* we are going to take a closer look inside ourselves. We are going to take a journey of the spirit. What really matters in this world isn't what other people are doing, or saying, or thinking; the only thing that really matters from the perspective of eternity is your spirit and what you allow it to become. The ancient wisdom goes that you should only work to change the things that you have the power to change. Any attempt to change things outside of your control is an exercise in futility.

When it comes to getting rid of the mean in your life, you have a couple of factors to deal with: yourself and the Mean Girl. Knowing that you have no power over her but a great deal of power over yourself, it stands to reason that the bulk of your effort should be in that direction—inward. And so *Mean Girls Gone* is a tool just for you. In

this small book you will not find what
you found in *Mean Girls*. This isn't a line-
by-line guide to managing the Mean Girl.
It isn't a list of ways to react to her or things
to say to her. Instead, it's a trip through the inner
workings of your heart and soul. To help you make
that trip, I have included journal pages. They will help
you delve deep into your heart and see what lies hidden
that might be adding to your emotional turmoil of living
with mean. Use these pages as an exercise in spiritual
honesty. Risk making a change that will impact your mind
and emotions.

What I hope you find in these pages is truth—the truth
that will shine the light of eternity on your spirit and give
you wings to rise above the mundane and morbid aspects
of life with a Mean Girl nipping at your heels. Read this
book however you desire. From front to back, back to
front, or somewhere in between. Read it daily, nightly,
weekly, whatever your soul desires, but read it and test
it. See if the truth contained inside these pages doesn't lift
your spirit and help you to see things from a more divine
perspective. This book can be done solo or with a close
friend, but either way, risk honesty. Dare to dive deep inside
yourself and discover the part of your soul that yearns for
peace with the maker of the universe.

Do you have a Mean Girl problem?

If you aren't sure if this book is for you or not, give this a try. Take the following quiz and see if you have a Mean Girl problem that needs some spiritual salve.

Answer the following:

Do you have a Mean Girl in your life?   Yes   No

Have you been dumped for another girl?   Yes   No

Do you mainly have guy friends?   Yes   No

Have you been mad at a girl in the past
    two weeks?   Yes   No

Has a girl 3-way called you?   Yes   No

Has a girl ever gossiped about you?   Yes   No

Has a girl tried to steal your boyfriend?   Yes   No

Do you do all you can to avoid girls 'cuz they're just
    plain mean?   Yes   No

If you answered yes to two or more of these, you probably have a Mean Girl problem. This guide is designed to help you understand God's will for you when it comes to your Mean Girl. He has something to say to you about her and, more importantly, about you. And my hope is that his will won't be such a mystery any longer after you take a walk through *Mean Girls Gone*.

Selah.

This book starts with you and ends with you. That's why you will find here some journal pages aching to be filled in by you. (Later on, some of the journal pages will just be blank for you to write down any thoughts you need to. But this time I'm going to give you a few questions to help you get started.) Before you dive into the truth about mean, take some time to do a spiritual inventory of yourself. It will do you good to think about what your soul is crying out for and what you hope to find within yourself as you take this journey. So open up your heart and look into the inner workings of your soul.

What is missing from your
spiritual life right now?

Describe the spiritual life
that you'd like to have.

Are you willing to allow a change in your heart and mind in order to relieve the pain of mean? What's more, are you willing to work to free your spirit from the Mean Girl's bondage?

What 3 things will you commit to do in the next week that will draw you closer in your relationship with God (journaling, meditation, prayer, reading, etc.)?

What 3 things bother you the most
about your Mean Girl problem?

How would you like to act
around Mean Girls in the
future? Are there ways you have
acted in the past that you wish
you could erase?

What is your goal
when it comes to your
Mean Girl problem?

What do you want from this book? Why did you pick it up? What do you want to be changed in your life when you're done reading it?

List 2 girls you will pray for while you are reading this book:

If you have a friend or 2 who might benefit from this same journey you are taking, list them here. Then talk to them about doing this study with you. Being vulnerable and reading your journaled thoughts to each other will help you both to dig deeper into your souls and clean out the muddy parts.

It is
impos

to enter into communion with God when you are in a **critical temper;** it makes you

sible

hard
and **vindictive**
and **cruel,**

and leaves you with the flattering unction that you are a superior person.

—Oswald Chambers

Freeing Your Soul from the Bondage of Mean

What other girls think of you cannot determine your success

If what other girls think of you could determine your success in life, you would be a failure in everything. There's no way in the world every girl will like you or what you do. You can't let that bother you. Even if they think your dreams are stupid and your thoughts are nonsense, they can't be your gauge for achievement or happiness. Only you truly know what God has called you to do. Only you know the purpose God has given your life. How faithful would you be if you let every girl's opinion of your dreams change that very dream?

Remember this: if your dream in life isn't tested, you will never know if it is truly from God. Just like the refiner's fire sifts out the dross from the silver, your testing will sift out the fake dream from the true one. Instead of being *afraid* of the test of your dream, *look* for it. If it isn't there, then the dream itself is probably not from God, because anything he calls you to do has to be tested to be proven right and good.

Dive

1. Think about the dreams you have. Which of them has been the hardest to attain? Can you understand how a real dream has to be tested to prove itself? It's like *American Idol.* Their dream of being stars has to be tested every week by performing really hard music live in front of millions of people, but the ones who pass the test get the prize and see their dreams unfold in front of their eyes. What dream do you have that you are willing to have tested to prove it is good? Is there a dream that you just don't want to fight for? Then maybe that isn't a dream after all. Remember, *"the refining pot is for silver and the furnace for gold, but the Lord tests hearts"* (Proverbs 17:3 NASB).

2. Think about the Mean Girl in your life. How does she try to kill your dreams? Imagine her as a tool for your refining. The next time she does something to cut you down, think about it as another part of the proving ground, proving that you will not give up on who you are, on who you dream to be, or on the holiness you wish to attain.

3. Write out your dreams. Write down the things you are willing to go to the mat for. And then when the testing comes, thank God that he wants to help you be strong enough to live your dream.

Controlling what others think about you is a giant waste of time

The hardest thing in the world to overcome is thinking you have to control what other girls think about you. All your energy gets wrapped up in what they think. Are you nice enough, smart enough, cute enough, faithful enough? Do they think you're cool, insightful, honorable? Are you rich enough, good enough? You spend all your energy trying to look better to the rest of the world. But all of this is a waste of your time because what others think is not your responsibility. It is not even within your power. You have to fight the urge to justify and to position yourself in the eyes of others because it's taking away God's role. He'll justify. He'll take care of you. Trust the creator and peace will be yours.

Dive

1. Do you have a good or a bad self-image? Whatever you answered, it doesn't matter, because only what *God* thinks ultimately matters. A girl who understands that what *others* think about her and even what *she* thinks about herself doesn't ultimately matter is so led by her spirit that she is free to fail, free to make

mistakes, and free not to fit in. When you understand whose opinion *really* matters, you shine, and
the world will begin to notice. Today, change your
concerns about yourself into concerns about your
spirit. Where does its energy go? What does it focus
on? If you can't find beauty around you, then look
harder. God has placed it everywhere. Today, find
beauty outside yourself and thank God each time
you do.

2. How have you tried to justify yourself in the past
week? Did it work? Think about who you were trying to convince. Tell God today that you trust him
to be your shield and your fortress and that you will
no longer be concerned with outward appearances.
What is more important to you, being at peace or
being right?

3. *"Many are the plans in the mind of a man, but it is the
purpose of the* Lord *that will stand"* (Proverbs 19:21
ESV). You can plan and manipulate your life and
others' lives all you want, but in the end, who do
you think prevails? Whatever you plan or devise in
your mind, run it by the all-knowing mind of God.
Does it please him? If not, be ready to see your plans
changed.

A person without self-control
is as defenseless as a city
with broken-down walls.

—King Solomon
in the book of Proverbs,
chapter 25, verse 28 NLT

stop   breathe   think

Don't judge who you can't control

If the only thing you have control of is your-self, then complaining about other girls and their issues is not only wrong, it's destruc-tive. Constantly being occupied with things beyond your control leaves you feeling frus-trated and bitter. Sure, the mistakes of oth-ers may become more and more obvious the closer your spirit draws to heaven—but so will your own mistakes, so concentrate on those and leave others' improvements to them. Stop wrestling with thoughts of how bad they are and admit out loud that just by thinking like that you show yourself to be as bad as them. "Therefore you have no excuse, everyone of you who passes judgment, for in that which you judge another, you condemn yourself; for you who judge practice the same things" (Romans 2:1 NASB).

Dive

1. Complaining is so unattractive. No one likes to be around someone who finds fault with everything. Think about your world. Is it ugly, bitter, and resentful, or is it positive, hopeful, and energetic? If you are feeling worn out by the world, stop the complaining. The next time you get ready to complain, stop yourself and say something nice, something positive. Today is the day. Turn over a new leaf. Become Miss Positive and your spirit will soar.

2. You know that the only thing you have control of is yourself, so why not exercise a bit of self-control? Show your body and your mind who is in charge. Determine that you will change something today—an old habit, complaining, whining, an over-eating problem, an under-eating problem. God has given you the power; only your trust in that power is lacking. *"For God did not give us a spirit of timidity, but a spirit of power, of love and of self-discipline"* (2 Timothy 1:7). Change something about you that you thought you could never change, because what you can't change controls you. Remember, some say it takes 29 days to make a new habit, so buck up and take control of your body, your life, and your spirit. Don't give up and don't give in.

stop   breathe   think

Some estimate that over their 40 years of wandering, God allowed over 1 million of the children of Israel to die in the wilderness because of their complaining.

—Bowes, quoted in
The Encyclopedia of 7700 Illustrations

At the moment you blame, you lose control

We can make our plans, but the Lord determines our steps.

—the book of Proverbs*

When you blame other girls for what happens to you, you waste your energy and destroy your faith. Since it isn't what happens to you but what you think about what happens to you that matters, no one has the power to control your life. So blaming some girl for what happens to you is a waste of energy that only dilutes the power over yourself that God wants you to maintain. See, you can have no self-control as long as you are giving all the control over to some other girl who either intentionally or just accidentally manipulates you.

Truly healthy girls have no need to blame themselves or somebody else for their problems. Haven't you heard that God determines your steps, not you, or your friends, or even your enemies? How long will you allow a world that has no real power to have power over you?

Things happen. But don't let *things* control you, because you are a slave to whatever has mastered you.** To be a slave to anyone or anything other than God is complete disobedience to the 1st commandment—"have no other gods before me" (Exodus 20:3). Decide today to set your thoughts on what is good, and choose not to blame her for the steps that God has laid out for you.

Dive

1. Who have you given control of your life to? The best way to figure this out is to determine who you think about the most. Whoever occupies most of your thought time is the one in control of your life.

2. Who do you blame? Are there people in your life that you blame for your life? This is a position of weakness. You are giving control over to others when you think like this. No one can control your spirit or your mind but you, and in the end that's all that matters. A mind free to think on things of peace, hope, and light is a mind under control of no one but God. Today confess to God that you blame others. List them, and then set them free from blame. Decide that you and your God alone are in control of your destiny.

3. What do you have faith in? Is God big enough to carry your world? Or have you created a backup for him? Think about who runs your world.

4. Read the 10 commandments today. Get a Bible and find Exodus 20. Meditate on the age-old truth found inside of them. Do you believe it? Do you live it?

stop   breathe   think

Have you noticed?
When she gossips, she's
an evil cow, but when
you gossip, you're just
sharing with your friend.

Don't take rejection as insight on the will of God

In our attempts to figure out God's will for our lives, we often take any sign we can as the sign that God wants us to give up on something. "The door closed," we say. But the truth is, the opposite might be true. God has to test your dream for it to be proven authentic. Your calling has to be tested. In fact, if there isn't a battle to fight, then you must be doing something wrong. Progress requires resistance.

Check your vision. If there isn't someone, even a girl, trying to stop or dissuade you, then it's probably not the battle you need to be fighting.

Dive

1. Everybody has a dream, although they might be afraid to admit it. What is your dream? Have you told anyone? Have you considered if it is an honorable dream, one that you can be proud of? If it is, then watch for opposition. When you see resistance, simply smile and thank God that he finds you worthy of testing. Prove your dream is good by sticking to it even in the face of opposition. Ancient wisdom passed down through generations goes like this: "*The crucible for silver and the furnace for gold, but the LORD tests the heart*" (Proverbs 17:3).

   Check your opposition. Listen to what the Mean Girls say, consider it, and if there is a shred of good advice in what they say, take it. Practice harder, work longer, do what it takes to achieve that dream you have been entrusted with. This week write down 2 things that you will work on to bring you closer to your dream.

No one can insult you

Girls might try to insult you. They might accuse you or even abuse you, but it isn't the girl herself who hurts you. It's how you think about the insult that determines if you will be hurt or not. You can choose to ignore the statement or even to think about where the person is coming from. But they can't hurt you unless you choose to take it that way, because it is never the thing itself but how you decide to think about the thing that hurts.

Dive

1. Today, write about a girl who insulted you or cut you down—but write about the incident from her perspective. Try to imagine what she was feeling that would make her do what she did.

2. Consider how you can think about what she said or did in a different way. What she said can't physically hurt you, so it's what you are thinking that hurts. Write down 3 things about this event that you could use for your good. Try to find something positive to focus on instead of the bad part.

A rebuke impresses a man
of discernment more than a
hundred lashes a fool.

—Proverbs 17:10

Forgive over and over again

People are trying to do the best they can.

When a girl hurts you, mistreats you, or even acts in an evil way toward you, stop and think to yourself, *If I were her and in her place, I probably would have done the same thing. I don't know her history and her emotions, so I can't judge her actions toward me.* We don't know what God is doing in the people who hurt us. Time and again he uses these hurts for our good, but when we won't forgive or let it go, we lose the power he is offering us.

When people don't do what you want them to do, exercise the gift of forgiveness and say, "Oh well, may God's will be done." Then let it go. Don't start to look at yourself in the light of her snide remarks or evil actions, and don't even compare yourself to that perfect girl you are wanting to be. Growing more holy is gradual. You fall, you get back up; you fall, you get back up.

When you forgive others over and over again, you begin to experience the peace of God. And peace is this: "You keep him in perfect peace whose mind is stayed on you, because he trusts in you" (Isaiah 26:3 ESV).

Dive

1. Forgiveness doesn't mean forgetting; it just means moving on and choosing not to hold a grudge. When you refuse to love someone because of something evil they did, you refuse to forgive them. And unforgiveness will eventually eat you alive. Make a list of the people you haven't forgiven, and decide today to forgive them. Tell God that you are sorry and that you are forgiving them. If you need to, make some time to hang out with them and, if they are aware that you are holding a grudge, set them free by telling them you are over it.

2. How many times are you willing to forgive her? Consider the teachings of Jesus Christ, who told the men who followed him, "and if he sins against you seven times **in the day**, and turns to you seven times, saying, 'I repent,' you must forgive him" (Luke 17:4 ESV, emphasis added). Can you imagine forgiving someone 7 times in 1 day? If I stepped on your foot 6 times, and each time I said I was sorry, how would you react to the 7th time? Are you willing to forgive girls who hurt you? Girls who don't even know they hurt you? The key is to get over it. Not everything is an insult or an evil act. So don't take yourself too seriously. If they haven't committed a sin, then maybe you just need to move on and forget about it.

stop   breathe   think

Have you noticed? When she takes a lot of time to do something, she gets on your nerves, but when you do, you are just being careful.

Friends are essential for a healthy spiritual life

Community, aka friendship, is the key to managing your spiritual life and your Mean Girl problem. Without a concerted effort to make and keep friends, you become more and more a victim of the whims of the Mean Girl and the deterioration of your spirit. It is crucial to develop healthy relationships that feed your spirit and nurture your emotions. The trials and joys of friendship are how we learn to sail on rough waters and keep the boat afloat. If you demand perfection from someone before they can be your friend, you will forever be friendless. Allow people to be human, forgive them, love them, and protect them, and they will protect you from the slings and arrows of the Mean Girl.

Dive

1. How many friends do you have? If you can't really claim any, then make a plan for who you will pursue. Begin to be nice to them. Ask them to do things with you. Care about them. Find at least 2 good friends that you can look to for support and companionship. If you already have friends, then make sure you are taking care of them. There is power in numbers, so don't let yourself become a lone wolf, or you'll be an easy target for the Mean Girl.

2. Unforgiveness can fester like an open wound if left alone for long. Make a list of the people in your life that you believe you have not forgiven, and confess to God today that you will forgive them. When you do this you will notice that you stop spending so much time thinking about them, worrying over them, and wishing they were gone. Your spirit will be free the moment that you forgive.

stop breathe think

Have you noticed? When she nags people about their flaws, she is being critical and witchy, but when you do, you're just being helpful.

Healing
from the
Inside Out

You grow the most
in the hard parts of life

Every difficult situation in life
offers you the opportunity to
access the strength of your spirit.
Instead of fearing your painful situations, try to look at them as a time
for strengthening. If you don't use your
muscles, they get weak and flabby. But a
muscle that gets used a lot is refined, lean,
and powerful. If you want more and more of
the fruit of the Spirit in your life, you have to
exercise those fruits, and it is in these fiery trials
that you get the opportunity to do just that. Are
you being tested? Call on the gift of patience. Are
you tempted by something you really want but
shouldn't have? Then call upon self-control.
Use these trials as opportunities to grow
your fruit into the powerful tools that
were designed for you.

Dive

Here is a list of the fruit of the Spirit, tools that strengthen you and bring you to a place of healing and wholeness. Some might seem hard to live out, but for a healthy spirit they are crucial. Read Galatians 5:22–23.

love

joy

peace

patience

kindness

goodness

faithfulness

gentleness

self-control

stop   breathe   think

If suffering is completely in God's hands, don't we just leave it up to His will? Why don't we believe that, just as He can bring us back to a trial when we run away, He can also protect us when we don't run away?

—Tertullian

What you have lost has merely been returned to where it came from

Do not worry about losing what you think you own, because in the truest sense of the word, you don't own anything. Everything belongs to God to do with as he sees fit. Nothing owned by Job belonged to Job,* and nothing belongs to you. So instead of feeling angry or hurt because of what has been taken from you, just tell yourself that it has been returned to God to care for and redistribute or protect. Don't be angry with the girl who has taken it from you. It's not your job to decide who God uses for what purpose. Instead, be like a traveler who rents a room in a hotel and cares for it while she stays but returns it to the owner as she goes on her way.

* See the Old Testament book of Job for more info on the guy.

Dive

Let go. If someone who you think is yours has turned against you or been taken from you, rethink your position. Spend some time in prayer allowing God to take back what is really his. If you want to, close your eyes, imagine the person, and imagine walking up to God and leading this person into his arms. Then imagine turning and walking away, trusting God to do what he wants with the person.

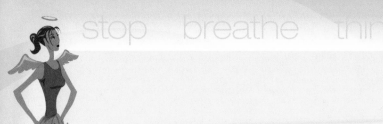

stop   breathe   think

Avoid the cares and anxieties of this world

Avoid the cares and anxieties of this world, because **they are just momentary distractions from your real purpose.** To allow them to consume you is to take your focus off your goal, the prize for which you were made. Beware of returning to what you renounced. Before you took on the Spirit of the Lord, you managed your world with all of your energy, and now you have to resist the urge to go back into that same state of mind. If you did, you would be like the man who was carrying a heavy load when he was picked up by a kind farmer in a cart. The farmer offered him a ride and helped him on board, but as they rode on, the man with the load continued to struggle to keep it on his shoulders. "Why don't you let down your load since I have picked you up?" asked the farmer. "Oh, it was so nice of you to pick me up," said the man with the load. "I couldn't burden you further with letting down my load." Don't be like that man. Trust the divine power of God, and allow him to lift your burden.

Dive

1. What are you carrying that is weighing you down? If you are living for your divine purpose, then you should feel light and airy, not heavy and burdened. Meditate on this truth. Think about the words of Christ, who said, "Come to Me, all who are weary and heavy-laden, and I will give you rest. Take My yoke upon you and learn from Me, for I am gentle and humble in heart, and **you will find rest for your souls**. For My yoke is easy and **My burden is light**" (Matthew 11:28–30 NASB, emphasis added). Will you be like the man in the wagon who still carried his load even though the wagon was underneath him?

2. Make a list of the things you will let go of today. Focus on your purpose and your holiness, and let the other things fall through the cracks, trusting him to pick them up. After you write the list, take it to a fireplace or some other safe place for burning and burn it, representing to yourself and to God how you will let go of controlling the things you can't control, the things that only make you crazy.

stop   breathe   think

If people aren't better for having known you, then you aren't loving them

But I say to you, Love your enemies and pray for those who persecute you.

—Jesus Christ*

Those who are holy understand that life isn't about them; it's about loving and serving the world, including the Mean Girls of the world. If you have a girl who is mean to you, then the holy thing to do is to care for her. What an honor, what a responsibility to be the big girl, the girl grown up, who knows that life is more than catfights and fitting in. It's about being true to yourself and honoring God by honoring his creation—even the Mean Girls. The winning soul is the one who is secure enough in her position in God's heart to know that persecution only makes her stronger, not weaker, and that fighting to be heard is weakness, not power. Confidence means having the strength to laugh in the face of insults and to know that in the grand scheme of things, they mean nothing.

* Matthew 5:44 ESV

Dive

1. Think about these words spoken by Jesus Christ: *"Love your enemies"* (Matthew 5:44). Do you have the strength of spirit to do that? If not you, then who does? He was talking to all of us, not just priests and nuns. Everyone who truly loves, loves those who hate them, for it's not real love to love only those who love you back. How will you love your enemy? What will you do this week that is loving? Turn the other cheek? Not retaliate? Not gossip? Not hate? What will you do to love?

2. Prayer works. Use it. Use it to pray for her. Pray that her spirit would be lightened and that her anger would subside. Pray for her every day this week—not for yourself, but for her good.

You don't have to feel good to have peace

Guys sometimes think girls are
crazy because we feel things so
deeply, but the truth is, we aren't crazy
because of what we feel but because of how
we act on our feelings. Feelings are healthy to
some extent. They help us understand our wants
and sometimes our needs. But the trouble comes when
we think that if we don't feel good all the time, something is terribly wrong. The truth is, it's normal to just
feel awful sometimes. When you feel depressed, it doesn't
always mean it's the end of the world. Sometimes it's just
a season. It's just a hormone. It's just an empty stomach
or mind. Don't lie to yourself and believe that you have to
feel good all the time to be normal. Every woman in the
world feels crappy sometimes. The thing to remember is
that feelings aren't reality, and they don't always have to
be analyzed ("What's wrong with me?") or obeyed ("I'm
feeling depressed, so I won't go to school today").
Sometimes the brain has to take over and deny the
emotion any territory. It can be there, but you
don't have to listen to it like it's the gospel

truth. Especially when it comes to hormones—sometimes they just mess with you and get you feeling all kinds of weird things. Just do what I do: tell yourself, "This will pass." I find that when I simply remember that everything is temporary when it comes to feelings, I am much happier. The worst thing to do is to think it will never change—to think, "I'll always feel yucky!" It isn't true, so don't buy the lie.

Dive

Write about your yucky feelings. Describe them like a good journalist. Look at them objectively and write about the truth. Remember when you felt good and the last time you felt bad. Then remember when that bad feeling ended. Do what you can to convince yourself that feelings can't run your life.

stop   breathe   think

If a habit is bad, don't feed it

Habits are the creation of repeated action. They grow or drop off based on repetition. If you make it a habit to read, you will become a better reader. If you regularly exercise, you will become stronger. It's the same with your spirit. Whenever you are envious, you strengthen your envy. You nurture it and grow its power in your life.

If you don't want to live with envy, then don't continue to feed it every time it pops up. Give it nothing to support its life. If you will forsake it and end the repetition of envy, even if you can only do it every other time, it will slowly get better. Soon you'll have a day of avoiding it, then a week of avoiding it, and eventually the harmful emotion will be replaced by a healthier one.

Dive

If envy isn't your sin of choice, then what is? Pick something that plagues you, that makes you feel depression, anger, resentment, loneliness, or jealousy, and then do what this exercise says: stop feeding it. Turn it off at every chance. Change the channel, move on to another subject, get out of the environment that is causing it. Each time you do this, you will weaken its grip on you.

Things appear difficult to us only when we don't remember God.

—Chrysostom

stop breathe think

Girls are essential to life

How do you feel about girls? Do you trust them? Are they generally nice? Think about your feelings toward girls in general. When you walk into a room and see two tables, one with mainly girls and one with mainly guys, which table do you go to? Why?

Other girls are essential to your life. You might think that right now guys "get you," but the only one who will ever truly "get you" is another girl. Guys can never completely understand how you feel, no matter how much they say they do. They don't feel the way we do. They don't have the same hormones coursing through their veins; they don't have the same things in life happening to them. They'll never have cramps or a baby. They're just different—good, but different.

Every girl should have a least 1 good girlfriend she can trust. One she can spend the night with and talk to till 4 in the morning. One she can call when she's crying or when she's sick. If you'd like to have more girlfriends and fewer Mean Girls in your life, then think about how you feel about girls. If you don't trust them, they'll never trust you. Sometimes you have to risk being hurt in order to find friendship.

Dive

Today, write about how you feel about girls. What you feel when you see them walking down the hall. How they make you feel when they talk, when you laugh together, when they rub your back. Write about the good in girls and the bad in girls. How can you start to accept the bad so you can get to the good?

We cannot clearly and properly know God unless the knowledge of ourselves be added.

—John Calvin

Finding
Inner Peace
in the Face
of Mean

The way to peace
is acceptance

The way to peace is acceptance. Accept the
things that happen to you as allowed by God.
This doesn't mean you have to resign yourself to a miserable existence, but don't get
angry when things don't go your way. Things
go as things go. Accept them and move on.
You can make no forward motion without
first accepting what has happened and then
moving beyond it to a place free from your
attachments. Don't get angry when you don't
get your way. Know that things are as they
are and the only thing in your control is how
you choose to remember them. Will they be
the things that destroyed you or the things
that made you? A soul set free knows that
"God causes everything to work together for
the good of those who love God and are
called according to his purpose for
them" (Romans 8:28 NLT).

Dive

1. Have you accepted the things that have happened in your life? Or do you fight against them? Hate them? Hate your life? If you want peace—true, undying peace—then practice accepting the things that you cannot control. Your parents' divorce, your brother's attitude, the Mean Girl. Trust that God knows what he is doing, and through that find inner peace.

2. If you have a grudge against someone who controls your life, like a teacher or a parent, release them today. They have control over you simply because God allows them to have control. The sooner you let go of trying to manipulate those who ultimately have the final say, the sooner you will be free to just be.

The affliction
of affection

We are afflicted by affection **when we become addicted to the need for it.** Affection from others cannot be the object of your attention. It shouldn't concern you if other girls like you or not. If you are acting in accord with your faith, you can't become preoccupied with what she thinks of you. Once you are determined that everyone has to like you, you are controlled by that desire more than by God. You become a victim of your need for affection. The truly spiritual girl is so concerned with pleasing God that she can't become preoccupied with human attention. And her mantra becomes, "seek first the kingdom of God and his righteousness, and all these things will be added to you" (Matthew 6:33 ESV).

Dive

1. Addiction = a compulsive need for something. What addicts you? What things in your life today do you feel that you just must have? Do you have to have people liking you? How do you feel when a girl doesn't like you? Is your feeling healthy, or can you choose to change the way you think and reduce your addiction?

2. A girl concerned about pleasing God has little time to worry about pleasing people. Would you like freedom from the stress of peer pressure and the need to fit in? Find out what pleases God and go after that with all your energy this week. When it comes to your Mean Girl, pick up *Mean Girl: Facing Your Beauty Turned Beast* and find out what God requires of you.

3. This week try being more concerned with helping girls than with helping yourself to feel good. Each time you feel left out, alone, or hurt, turn that off and tell yourself, "Not myself but serving others, that is my goal this week." You will soon find that a girl who isn't focused on herself is a happier girl.

stop   breathe   think

Have you noticed?
When she doesn't like your friends, she's being mean, but when you don't like hers, you're just a good judge of character.

Refuse to be controlled

Faithfulness is repeatedly, as much as you have to, refusing to be controlled by things outside of your control. It is impossible to remain faithful to your calling if you think that things outside your control are inherently evil. If you concentrate on the evil in things or people, you will create the habit of blaming circumstances and others for your problems rather than believing that God works all things together for your good. You will allow those things outside your control to, in effect, control you.

Dive

Think about your favorite movie or book. Think about how things seemed hopeless for the hero or heroine but in the end it all came together for their good. Life is like this if we allow ourselves to see the bigger picture. What seems like hell right now might just be a setup for a life of heavenly bliss.

Practice indifference
to circumstances

God offers you freedom. And part of that freedom is found in letting go of things you can't control, like other people, circumstances, and events. You can't be filled with joy and the love of God if you are constantly filled with fear and ambition.

Do you want to be more than a conqueror? Then don't enter into battles that you have no control over. Pray instead, and let God fight those fights for you. There are three areas where your freedom is found: your will, your interpretation of events, and the use of your thoughts. In these areas you have complete control. And in these same areas you will find your freedom from fear, worry, and manipulation.

Your joy in life is always independent from your circumstances. Faithfully determine to be indifferent to your circumstances and the Mean Girl and instead to be like the apostle Paul, who learned to be content whatever the circumstances (Philippians 4:11). The only way to do that is to determine to live by that which you *can* control: your thoughts, your prayers, your actions, and your will. And then know that all those things *outside* of your control are not yours to manage. Trust that what God allows to happen to you and around you is within his divine will.

Dive

1. Make a list of the things you can control. Be honest—if you can't control them, then don't write them in the control list.

2. Now make a list of things that you can't control but wish you could (i.e., people, events, weather).

3. Look at those lists and cross out everything on the second one, all the things you can't control. Each time one of those things begins to bother you or hurt you, tell yourself, "I can't control that, so I won't fight it." You will be free when you truly realize the things you can't control and let go of trying to control them.

stop   breathe   think

Have you noticed?
When she has an
amazing outfit on, she
is showing off, but
when you do, you are
just fashionable.

stop   breathe   think

Fear is the fuel of faith

The truly victorious soul is the one who has learned to conquer self. You have power only when you do what you don't want to do and risk what his Word dares you to risk. Your biggest loss is when you give in to the whims of fear, emotion, and worry. But your biggest win is when you refuse to let feelings rule your life. You gain ground in the battle for peace in life if you practice self-denial, and by that I mean if you stand in the face of your negative feelings like fear and say, "No, I'm not gonna hide from life to protect you."

The spiritual girl doesn't demand peace of herself, but she stands in the face of trials and tribulation and refuses to be moved by them. The pain might sting and the fear might scream, but she will not be moved because she responds only to the Spirit and not to the flesh.

Remember what he said: "Be still, and know that I am God" (Psalm 46:10).

Dive

1. What feelings control you most? What are the top 3 things that you feel the most overwhelmed by? Fear, worry, anger, loneliness? When you let emotions control your decisions and your actions, you lose peace. Decide today which emotions you will choose not to obey. Then the next time you feel them, remind yourself that they are only feelings, not fact, and turn to God for truth.

2. Oswald Chambers put it best when he said, "My goal is God Himself, not joy nor peace, nor even blessing, but Himself, my God." People who struggle for peace don't often find it, but people who give up and allow those things they can't control to happen unwittingly find themselves in that same peace they thought they had to clamor for. I find that when my goal is God himself, rather than the peace I crave, God's presence soothes my soul and I have all I ever needed.

stop breathe think

Have you noticed?
When she does really well in class, she's a brownnoser, but when you do, you're a good student.

Think upon the divine,
not the trial

A spiritual mind has learned to think about the divine in times of trial rather than think on the trial itself. With the first impulse of anger or rage, the spiritual mind removes itself from the situation and looks to the divine, the author and perfecter of our faith. The Mean Girl in your life can be used by God to see if you will remove your eyes from him. The disciplined soul teaches itself, by doing it over and over again, to return its eyes heavenward even though every temptation is to the opposite direction. Though the Mean Girl demands your attention or the trial seems to demand your worry or fear, you must keep focused on him. In this continual denial of our own urge to panic or fight back, the spirit is perfected and grown more into the likeness of the divine.

Dive

1. As author John Eldredge says, you are part of an epic, part of a story so much bigger than you've ever dreamt or imagined. Think about some of your favorite movies, ones like *Titanic, Braveheart, The Lord of the Rings,* and *Gladiator,* and notice the epic nature of the

stories. The reason we love these stories is because they resemble ours. The trials the characters must face are epic, dangerous, treacherous. But we can see the big picture; we understand that they must pass through the trials and the testings to bring the epic to completion. Try to think of your life like an epic movie—each trial, each mess thrown at you by the Mean Girl is merely another scene that you must bravely travel through in order to get to the prize, the goal of your life.

2. Watch your favorite drama or adventure movie this week and take note of all the trials the hero must go through to save the day. If the hero refused the test or cowered in the corner, would the movie be as good? Think about your life and how your traumas compare. Do you want to survive? Do you want to fight the good fight? Then remember that the spiritual soul looks heavenward, not down to the cause of the pain but up to the author of our perfection.

3. When the world throws you a punch, remind yourself, as the apostle Paul reminds us, that you can be "beaten, and yet not killed; sorrowful, yet always rejoicing" (2 Corinthians 6:9–10).

Have you noticed?
When she spends a lot, she's a spoiled brat, but when you do, you're just treating yourself to a much-deserved gift.

Ignore the unimportant

Spiritual perfection requires that you seek only what is important and ignore everything else. It is actually good to be ignorant of things that don't concern you, because they aren't your purpose. The pursuit of trivial things like what your Mean Girl thinks or says about you is a distraction from your focus. Concentrate on faith and those things God asks of you. Trying to change a Mean Girl only distracts you from your purpose. Stay focused. And check yourself when you start to get important in the eyes of others. Pride can sneak up on you if you aren't continually keeping your motives and focus in check.

Dive

Make a list of those important things in life. What is your focus today? What do you have to do that can't be manipulated or controlled by the Mean Girl? Make this a list that matters: love, hope, peace. Concentrate on what you want and what God wants for you, not on the distractions she might throw your way.

stop   breathe   think

stop   breathe   think

God allows everything

Most of us don't consider that both good and bad things pass through the hands of God. If you can realize that both help and harm come to you because God allows them to, then you can stop blaming people and situations. Each thing, whether good or bad, is there because he has allowed it, and he will use it for your good if you will look toward him and not toward the earthly thing that brought it. When you do this you no longer need the approval of others, and their lies and vicious gossip have little or no effect on you.

Dive

1. If it's true that both bad and good are allowed by God, then shouldn't we thank him for both the bad and the good? Today take 5 minutes to thank God for your trials, your Mean Girls, and your bullies and ask him what glory he would get out of this.

2. Make a list of the Mean Girls in your life, and every morning for the next week, pray for them. As you do, thank God that he has given you the ability to love the way he does and to care more for others than for yourself.

The Lord doesn't allow
unthankful people to
have peace.
                    —Athanasius

stop   breathe   think

The End
of the
Journey

NOW LEAVING
MEANVILLE

Mean or not mean, that is the question

Look at the following list and score yourself, with 1 being totally not you and 10 being exactly you.

When someone hurts me, I can forgive them.

1   2   3   4   5   6   7   8   9   10

I don't like getting revenge.

1   2   3   4   5   6   7   8   9   10

I never gossip.

1   2   3   4   5   6   7   8   9   10

No pain, no gain.

1   2   3   4   5   6   7   8   9   10

God has a reason for everything.

1   2   3   4   5   6   7   8   9   10

Life isn't fair and that's okay.

1   2   3   4   5   6   7   8   9   10

Not everyone has to like me.

1   2   3   4   5   6   7   8   9   10

Score:

35 or higher: *Bravo, fair one.* You have done well. Your spirit is bright and so is your outlook on life, faithful one. But if you didn't get a perfect 70, you might still have some areas to work on in order to bring ultimate peace into your life. Don't put this book away; keep it as a pick-me-up, a chance to bring refreshment to your staggering soul.

21–34: *Dark one,* come into the light. Living life on the verge of a pity party or anger fest doesn't bring you the peace that your soul longs for. Think about who you want to be and how you want to feel. If you are tired of being depressed and down a lot of the time, then maybe a more honest look inside at how you handle the mean in your life is still needed. You might want to give this book another read and let it seep into your pores a little more. It's never too late to refresh your tired spirit.

7–20: *Dear warrior,* not all of life has to be a fight. Remember, there is a bigger picture than you can see right now. All the energy you are spending in order to control your world is only spinning you out of control. You might not even realize it right now, but you are void of any peace and your spirit is withering from dryness. If you haven't read it yet, pick up a copy of *Mean Girls: Facing Your Beauty Turned Beast.* It might be just what you need to clear the cobwebs from your spirit.

For moral support or a virtual shoulder to lean on, check out www.meangirls.net.

As I said at the beginning, this book is about you from front to back. Hopefully you've had time to reflect, time to ponder, and time to dream. I pray that your soul is somehow lighter, more hopeful, and more determined. This has been a tough journey but one well worth the taking. Consider where you've come from and know where you are going. Take a look at the very first journal entry you made, your spiritual inventory, and now look at your life from the other side of the book. What have you learned? How have you changed? What will you do differently? Speak to your soul about life, love, and hope. Write your future. Commit to the possibilities of a deeper spiritual life.

How have you changed the way
you think about Mean Girls?

How could your
spiritual life be better?

What 3 things will you commit to do in the next week that will draw you closer in your relationship with God?

How will you act around Mean Girls in the future?

This exercise might seem a bit morbid, but bear with me. What I want you to do now is to think about the end of your life. How will the years you have spent on earth look to someone who lives long after you are gone? What will you have done, changed, and contributed to the world? As you think about this, you will begin to direct your steps for the future and begin to make purposeful decisions in all you do.

stop   breathe   think

Now think about your funeral. All your family and friends are there to say good-bye and remember the amazing you. Someone will give a eulogy, which is a testimony of your life, the things you accomplished and the people whose lives you touched. What I want you to do is to write your eulogy. In a paragraph or two, describe your life as if you were looking back over the years of a long life. What have you done? Who were you to people? How did you change lives? This exercise will set the pace for who you will become. Years ago in high school I did this same thing. I've since gone on to complete over half the things in my eulogy, including writing 5 books. Join me on a journey of the possible, and live a life defined by hope and love.

stop   breathe   think

Hayley DiMarco writes cutting edge books like *Mean Girls: Facing Your Beauty Turned Beast*, the best-selling *Dateable: Are You? Are They?*, *The Dateable Rules*, and *The Dirt on Breaking Up*, among others. Her goal is to give practical answers for life's problems and encourage people into stronger spiritual lives. Hayley has traveled the world with a French theater troupe, worked for a little shoe company called Nike, and created a multi-million dollar teen book business from scratch for Thomas Nelson Publishers. Hayley has seen a lot of life and decided to make a difference in her world. Hayley founded Hungry Planet, a think tank that feeds the world's appetite for truth through authors, speakers, and consultants. Hungry Planet helps organizations understand and reach the postmodern generation while Hungry Planet books tackle life's everyday issues with a distinctly modern voice.

For more info on Hayley and *Mean Girls: Facing Your Beauty Turned Beast*, check out www.meangirls.net.

For info on Hungry Planet, check out www.hungryplanet.net.

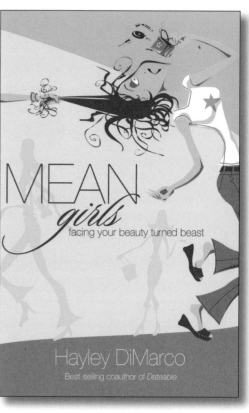